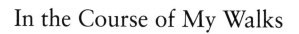

In the Course of My Walks

In the Course of My Walks

August Derleth

Edited by Richard Quinney

Borderland Books

Published by Borderland Books, Madison, WI
www.borderlandbooks.net

Published by arrangement with Arkham House Publishers, Inc., agent for April and Walden Derleth.

Publisher's Cataloging-In-Publication Data

Derleth, August William, 1909–1971.
[*Return to Walden West*. Selections.]

In the course of my walks / August Derleth ; edited by Richard Quinney ; wood-engravings by Frank Utpatel. — 1st ed.

p. : ill. ; cm.

Selections from: *Return to Walden West* / August Derleth. New York : Candlelight Press, [1970]

ISBN: 978-0-9815620-2-5

1. Derleth, August William, 1909–1971—Homes and haunts—Wisconsin—Sauk City. 2. Sauk City (Wis.)—Social life and customs. 3. Wisconsin—Intellectual life—20th century. 4. Authors, American—20th century—Biography. 5. Country life—Wisconsin—Sauk City. 6. Sac Prairie (Wis. : Imaginary place) I. Quinney, Richard. II. Utpatel, Frank. III. Title. IV. Title: Return to Walden West.

PS3507.E69 I5 2009
813/.5/209   2008942233

Wood engravings by Frank Utpatel

Printed in the United States of America
First edition

I wished to live deliberately, to front only the essential facts of life, and see if I could not learn what it had to teach, and not, when I came to die, discover that I had not lived.

— Henry D. Thoreau, *Walden*

Preface

AUGUST DERLETH begins his two Walden West books with the reasons for his life as an observer of things close to home. In *Walden West,* published in 1961, he writes the following Prologue:

A time came three decades ago, when I found I must choose between going out into the wider world or traveling widely in the microcosmos of Sac Prairie. I had been away from Sac Prairie scarcely half a year, immured in a city at editorial work, and I could ill bear separation from the village, the river, the hills, and the lowlands among which I had put down roots and with which I had come to terms of a sort: I walked the streets of the city many nights to assuage nostalgia for these familiar places, and I found nothing in the interminable round of concerts, plays, and parties to balance their loss.

When the opportunity came, I went back to Sac Prairie without regret. It did not matter that for a while my parents thought me a failure; they had endured before; they were patient enough to endure again. So I set about to write so that I might afford the leisure in which to improve my acquaintance with the setting and the inhabitants—hills, trees, ponds, people, birds, animals, sun, moon, stars—of the region I had chosen to inhabit, not as a retreat, but as a base of operations into a life more full in the knowledge of what went on in the woods as well as in the houses along the streets of Sac Prairie and in the human heart.

A decade later, in *Return to Walden West*, Derleth begins the book with an Apologia:

Long ago, during the years of my childhood, I was lost forever to the world in which men engaged life in momentous concerns and affairs, charmed away by the world intimately near to my senses

—of sunlight dappling a pond, the voice of running water, the matins of robins and mourning doves, the pensive threnodies of pewees and song sparrows, the majestic beauty of hawks aloft, the breathlessly exciting dance of woodcocks in the chill spring evenings, the shyness of violets and hepaticas, the arrogance of crows

—bewitched by the song of the hermit thrush and veery, by the wild nostalgia of killdeers and whippoorwills, by meadows yellow with cowslips or dusty rose with Joe-Pye weed, by hylas in April song and by fireflies in June, by the keening of screech owls in the night, by the lulling songs of toads in the spring ponds

—captivated by the wind's runes and the river's moods, by dew-hung grasses, lilacs and columbines, by the *redwing's early* conqueree, *by pussywillows and maple musk, by wild plum bloom crowding the woods' edges and the line-fences, by sunset and after-glow, new moon and evening star, by cloud and tree and hills, by pasture rose and coronilla, by rain and snow and nighthawks coasting down the buttes of sky, by wild geese aloft, by mosses and mushrooms in field and forest*

—and the solitudes of men and women who lived in this same world, as intimately near as I, and saw it seldom or never at all

—and all I did thereafter was done to enable me to live out that special enchantment and explore that world where the major concerns of other men did not matter—not fame or wealth or the pursuit of other phantoms conjured up by hope or love, valor or avarice.

For the remaining years of his life, Derleth would be true to his calling. He lived his life traveling the streets and byways of Sauk City, exploring the fields and woods and marshes along the Wisconsin River, in the environs of what he called "Sac Prairie." His writings, in fiction and nonfiction, would cover a wide range. But, always, there was the fidelity to the world of nature, the world in which he was most at home. Once again, from his writings in *Return to Walden West*, we are companions of August Derleth in the course of his daily walks.

— Richard Quinney

NOW AND THEN, in the course of my walks in the hills or marshes, there were brief periods when awareness of unity with all nature burgeoned—a sense of utter harmony with all things: leaf, stone, soil, blade, water, air—of kinship with insect, bird, all wild creatures—a pouring forth of secret springs deep within, filling me with an almost unbearable bliss. Every sense seemed heightened—I heard the distant hermit thrush as were it at my right hand—the fragrance of the maple leaves was never before so pervasive—I felt the wind as an intimate caress—I saw deep into the heavens in an experience that was both sensual and spiritual. I was one with the least grain of sand and the hawk soaring aloft, one with the mouldering log and the blossoming violet, one with the foraging muskrat and the greening slough, teeming with life—and one, too, with an invisible *anima*, a spirit of place and time knowing neither beginning nor end.

I was not at such times aware of body—or aware only as of something remote, separated from me, not an integral part of the ecstasy I felt. It was as if an instant, overwhelming communion had been established between the cells of my flesh and the molecules of all earth around me, and the sense of belonging intimately to my surroundings was integral to the moment. The sunlight shone within as well as on leaf or bole or the ground where I walked, as on the meadow and the hill with range of my sight, and the wind coursed through me as well as all around; a thousand voices cried out to me from outside, a thousand answered from within in a kind of mystic communion that was spontaneous and could never be brought voluntarily into being.

What its source was, I never knew, for it was associated with scores of small joys—hillside birch trees in blossom against an April sky of white cloud and blue heaven—a trillium nodding over the brook—a veery's song at morning—an osprey's high cross overhead—the rusty sheen off a redtail hawk wheeling in the sunlight—the new moon above the evening afterglow—sunlight dappling pond or stream—a song sparrow's threnody along the river—the crisp calls of crows on winter days—a field sparrow's ruminative song of a summer afternoon—the killdeer's first cry in spring—the soft cooing hoot of a long-eared swamp owl in the winter twilight—the dancing rapture of woodcocks against the April evening sky—the wild gyrations of jacksnipes aloft—and many more such moments of beauty poignant almost to the edge of pain. There were the aspects of earth that filled life with meaning, more ephemeral than the small span of human existence, more significant than the events most men account important, and often more lasting than love. And from these aspects arose those brief periods of ecstasy that made me one with all earth and sky, dust acknowledging dust in all the shapes into which dust is moulded from one state of being to another, season to season, generation to generation.

WE ARE COMMONLY TOO REMOTE from the stars and some of us are as isolated in the universe as any star in the limitless spaces outside our own universe; and we hear their very names—Arcturus, Altair, Antares, Betelgeuze, Rigel, Canopus, Vega, Sirius—as some unknown language, Greek or Russian or Chinese to one who can barely understand his native tongue. But we are as remote, too, from the forest of the grass and all the multitudes that inhabit it, as from the selvas and savannas in some distant land; and the insect that threads its way among the blades can no more be brought into our own narrow world than the stars can be brought down from overhead. We scarcely know our fellowmen, meeting them as wraiths that pass by dark, though they live in the same world and see the same stars and the same forests and never know the wildernesses inside and out.

For many of us the stars shine without being seen, our heads are turned so much earthward, toward our feet, and unseeing there; Venus or Jupiter or any other evening or morning star, Arcturus bringing up the spring, Antares a glowing coal in the southern heavens of summer nights, the Hunter striding by aloft, the Great Dog's blue-white eye looking out of the winter sky—all alike unseen, unknown, and the vast spaces stretching limitlessly away in all directions from the planet, as unrecognized, as unplumbed as the spaces within the confines of the mind. We are motes inhabiting a slightly larger mote in an incomprehensible vastness, hurtling toward infinity, though we commonly think ourselves gods, blind with vanity, and carrying destruction and death along our path, unaware of leaf or blade, fur, feather, insect wing. How can we know the stars when we are so commonly strange to the beauty and wonder of our own star?

Men have lost themselves, separated from nature, as had they cut off both arms and both legs, and blinded themselves until an ant and a blade of grass are no less remote than the stars. They move unseeing through beauty and wonder, dead and with the fear of death in them; the stars speak and the blades, the leaves, their fellow inhabitants in the forests of the grass and the trees speak, and they hear nothing but the hollow sound of their own voices. They are as separated from earth as from heaven, and engaged in concerns of no meaning in the cosmos, lost even to themselves as they were meant to be by nature, as remote from themselves as from the stars.

WALK OUT INTO FALLING SNOW, the soft, clinging flakes, and be lost and enclosed in an intimate private world by a natural phenomenon that borrows a little from the secret self and a little more from the fundamental mystery of the universe. The world of falling snow is related to that primitive awareness of concealment, which is always accompanied by an acceptance of and a desire to be hidden, akin to being enclosed by night and darkness. Here rather, it is not by darkness but by light, encurtained, as it were, from everything which had been but briefly before familiar and known.

Nothing in this white world is known; every familiar thing appears in strange guise; its inhabitants are creatures but briefly seen existing on a plane of equality with man as seldom at any other time—the foraging mouse, the resting deer, the darting rabbit, the industrious nuthatch. Trees looming over are spectral, no longer clearly defined; the sky is an infinity retreating, out of which the flakes descend in an endless cascade; you are in a cocoon of snow, and the prosaic everyday world is shut away.

And the silence! There is nothing equivalent to the silence of snow; all sound in the heart of a snowfall is muffled, distant, as unreal as the world beyond the wall of white. This too is an integral part of the falling snow, a world made up of silence, the endlessly falling flakes, the white strangeness, all lending a sense of the impermanence of things, of the alien within the confines of the known world, a kind of pleasant, reassuring strangeness, since you know that the familiar world lies just under the white blanket, just beyond the fall of flakes, just past the enclosing whiteness.

The backward flight to the womb, the return to the primitive urgence for wariness and concealment from the countless enemies of man's ancestors on the planet, the indulgence in the sense of solitude common to all men, the simple delight in the kind of beauty only a falling snow clinging to blade and leaf, to stone and man alike can afford—perhaps in one or all these lies the secret of this pleasure a man takes in being enclosed and locked away from the mundane world of every day by the intimate white flakes of this private world.

4

THE WHINE OF THE SAW-RIG was as much a part of winter in Sac Prairie as the English sparrows' social conversation at the grain elevator. Except on days of snow and bluster, it rose from one part of town after another from dawn to dusk as the men took the rig around to the piles of cordwood taken in during the autumn months, often in exchange for services or in trade. It was a companionable sound, one that made a kind of pulse in village life, despite all the snow and cold that diminished human activity in Sac Prairie in that frosty season.

There were three saw-rigs, variously owned, that came in from the country during the winter months and made the rounds. Many a lad heard the approaching whine with gloom and dismay for, however exciting it might be to watch, when it left there was work for him to do—at the least, to pile the chunks—at the most, to split the wood and then pile it, a task that seldom devolved upon me for I was anything but handy with an ax, and my father was firm in his conviction that I was as likely to cut off a leg as to split a chunk of wood, though piling it was not beyond me, and however much I might begrudge the time taken from a book being read, I took a certain pleasure in the fragrance of the newly-sawn wood that clouded the woodpile like a perfume from the summer woods.

I used to listen for the rising of the saw-rig's whine every winter. It came with mid-December, when cold finally made work in the fields impractical, as prelude to Christmas, announcing the season, as it were, with the promise of the holidays and snow that transformed the countryside into new vistas of singular character and beauty. It seemed to have an entity of its own, for all that it belonged to the machine and the men who operated it—a jocular crew, usually; it was a mellow sound, a steady, pleasant whine heard at a distance, less mellow when it was at hand, in one's own back yard or alley, where the connotation of all the physical labor it left in its wake perhaps helped to make it so.

In spite of the steady hum of the mill at the grain elevator, which made an incessant drone sometimes all day long throughout the year, it was the whine of the saw that seemed to be the voice of man's industry in Sac Prairie. Perhaps it was that the saw-rig involved men more directly than the impersonal mill, or that it was propelled from place to place, whereas the mill's voice rose steadily from but its building beside the railroad tracks in the heart of the village, and diminished as one moved away from it, scarcely heard at all at the perimeter of town, whereas the whine of the saw carried far beyond the streets of Sac Prairie, out into the country and across the Wisconsin into the hills.

But in the inexorable passage of years and the changes they brought, ever less wood was burned in village stoves and furnaces, as coal and electricity, oil and gas came to be more widely used, and at least the familiar saw-rig seldom came into town, and the whine of the saw was heard no more.

5

DOWN ALONG THE NORTH SLOPE of the Ferry Bluff, Walter Moely's sugar bush came to life late every winter—an extensive grove of very old and very young soft maple trees growing away from the hill into the bottomland along Honey Creek where it wound through the woods to the Wisconsin. At its edge, where the road passed along the base of the hill, stood the syrup camp—a sturdy cabin backed with rows of wood collected and piled there during the summer and autumn months against the maple syrup season, which began with soft weather any time in February or March and lasted often as long as six or eight weeks, depending upon the vagaries of the weather and the stamina of Walter Moely, a lean, taciturn, laconic man, one of few words, who had for many years made maple syrup there and took pleasure in doing so, though his labors often stretched far into the night and, once the sap was cooking, kept him constantly alert getting in wood, firing, settling the boiling sap, testing and drawing off the syrup.

There was something about this solitary occupation that drew me to the sugar bush, particularly at night—perhaps for its reflection of time past, for nothing here had changed very much save perhaps in the bush, where around some of the great old maples tubing had replaced some of the spiles. But the pails still hung from the trees, hundreds of them, glinting in the moonlight, and, walking among the trees, I would hear the sap dripping from the spiles as the sound of bells far beyond the horizon; and the sap cooked and bubbled and frothed in the shallow pans, filling the cabin with fragrance, and sending great gouts of steam through the vents in the roof; and the fire glowed whenever Walter opened the stove and put in more wood; and the sparks flew upward among the budded trees to be lost among the stars. Here, deep in the woods, isolated among the ancient boles, life burgeoned every winter, sometimes with snow still deep on the ground. Far to the north passed the highway, and the lights of farms shone across the meadows between the sugar bush and the highway, but here in this solitary place one man's industry turned all the hidden sweetness of the maples into fragrant steam and delicately flavored syrup and succulent sugar, an industry little changed from what it had been many decades before. A century ago men had turned the sap of the maple trees into sugar and syrup in much the same manner; and now this singular occupation continued unchanged, one of the last to defy mechanization—the work of a man's hands, with the aid of wood, fire, and the taste and judgment of the syrup-maker.

I used to stand in the cabin while the sap cooked, drinking in its fragrance, warmed by the heat of the fire, watching Walter go about his tasks, which allowed him little time to stand and exchange words now and then, feeling an ancient kinship with wood and fire and bubbling sap. Two centuries ago Indians had cooked sap and made sugar into mococks perhaps in this very place, though they were likely to have been less patient than Walter and sought out sugar or hard maples, instead of the soft from which more sap needed to be drawn for every gallon of syrup. But the syrup Walter Moely made always seemed to me to have a greater delicacy of flavor than that from hard maples and, taken warm from the pan, it was an ambrosia without peer.

What drew me there, night after night in the season was the solitude, the tangibility of spring in the sap surging upward to drop from the spiles into the buckets, making a little night music there, the tenuous continuity with time past, and even, at leave-taking, the sparks riding into heaven. I used to watch, standing outside the cabin, how the sparks rode the draft from the chimney, charging aloft among the maple branches hanging over, driving toward the amber eye of Arcturus shining there on many evenings, brief stars rising through the smoke and steam, red and yellow, only to wink out against the dark, while owls and foxes were abroad in equal wonder at what went on here so far from the haunts of men.

6

THERE WAS ALWAYS A TIME in May when the village and all the country around was taken over by the plum trees, most of them wild, their blossoms bursting suddenly on their dark limbs, before the leaves had unfurled; great drifts of plum bloom spilled fragrance to the wind and shone along the streets and lanes, leaning over into the alleys of Sac Prairie, marking the line-fences in the country, foaming at the edge of woods and on the hill slopes for miles along the country roads.

I stood often beside the plum groves, intoxicated by their perfume, which had no counterpart in woods or village, or I sat in their shade to read of a spring afternoon on a hill, but my attention usually wandered; something there was in the wild plum trees that sent my thoughts wool-gathering, something of such pristine beauty as seduced me happily alike from print and blank page I hoped to fill, something akin to the April new moon's promise among the budding trees, and the vermilion dawn, and the murmur of a brook that filled the hours with music, something like the soft flowering of the arc-lights over village street corners at night, stretching in limitless lines of yellow globes toward the afterglow west over the prairie, promising some memo-rable adventure just around the next bend, not of the body at all, but of the spirit, something that brought me close to the ultimate harmony of man and earth and the common bond shared by everything in the universe, all things sentient and alive, all things still and dead, past, present, and time to come.

But in time the plum trees retreated to the deep woods, with now and then a bright cloud of bloom at the edge of an alley or a village garden where no one had cut them away, rousing the old longing, the rootless desire to know the unknowable, to experience that which lies just beyond the rim of the known, to be taken into the very core of life, but this happens less often now than in the days of my youth — not alone because of the shame-ful despoiling of the roadsides and the line-fences, but because the young are forever near to the unknowable, and the aging are blinded to it by the very press of life even as they move toward death, its final ecstasy.

AMONG THE PERFUMES OF THE SPRING NIGHT, the exhalation of soft maple blossoms is almost lost, so delicate is it, so elusive in March and April evenings, one with the unfolding leaves, surrounding the trees where they stand like great yellow tapers in the evening, the thousands of fragile blossoms almost spectral on heaven at certain moments of the dusk—as in the early morning sunlight the trees reflect the sun with warmth and light of their own.

No one who knows the pervasive musk of maple bloom and leaves goes unaware of it. This vague essence is so transient that it is literally dependent on the humidity and the stillness of the air for one's awareness of its existence; in dry, windy air, no hint of it reaches the nostrils, even in a grove of blossoming trees; but in damp, still air, the musk clouds the places where the trees stand. I used to go into the marshes along the brook, cross the railroad embankment, and stand to write some verses in a grove of soft maples, drinking in the fragrant musk that descended from the unfolding leaves and the blossoms, a musk that blends with the smells that rise from the spring earth, of wet places, of opening soil, of scores of small plants pushing up out of the ground throughout the marshes, of the faint perfume of pussywillow and alder catkins.

The evasive fragrance of the soft maple is all but lost in hot summer weather, but of autumn nights the fallen leaves give off the same sweet musk — now the fragrance of death — and on October nights of rain especially the musk of soft maple leaves trodden underfoot along the village streets and country lanes is unmistakable to all who know it.

The musk of soft maples is the first spring fragrance to spread into the air, and the sweetest. Before isolating its source, I thought of it as simply the smell of growing things — an exhalation of the soil itself, of decaying wood, of opening leaves, of hidden blossoms — but the musk of moist spring days in late March and April is primarily that of the unfurling leaves and the more delicate perfume of the blossoms, spilling into the often chill air with its promise of the vernal season to come.

IN THE FIELDS AND HEDGEROWS away from the village in spring rose the pensive song of the field sparrow. From April into October the song came to ear—a sequence of strong, arresting notes, followed by a mellow diminuendo.

Largely lost in the medley of spring song, it came into its own in summer; it was a constant summer voice that never failed. I used to hear it rising at regular intervals from the fields east of the hills where I lay reading or writing of a summer afternoon—pleasant, intimate, as if it sounded for my ear alone. Song sparrows spilled their threnodies along the river below the hill and redwings sang from the willows there, crows cawed going by and the killdeer's wild crying rang out from time to time, but only the field sparrow sang steadily, and its voice came always from the fields on the slopes east of the hills. Neither stifling heat nor the disturbance of an approaching storm diminished that song, and no other rose from the fields save the occasional song of a lark, or fell more sweetly to the listening ear, a song of serenity that said all was well in this corner of the earth, a lulling melody that spoke for the grain waving and ripening in the summer sun.

Now and then I heard the field sparrow in the marshes, but not often, for the fields and pastures were his demesne; it was there he lived and foraged and raised his brood, and he never ventured far from them. On rare occasions I heard that familiar song in Sac Prairie—rising from some large open space resembling his favorite terrain. Walking out along the lane toward the prairie I came within his range, and heard him all the way through open country beyond old Mrs. Block's house, the last on the edge of the village, filling the summer afternoons with his ruminative threnody that never varied. I never heard it without a lifting of the heart, a quickening of the pulse, for it was as if I heard the voice of the countryside itself, the very pulse and throbbing of life in the fields.

OH, THE WILD CHERRY TREES that on a day in May opened their blossoms to spill their ineffably sweet perfume to the sunlit air, in the village and beyond the limits of Sac Prairie, clouding the roadsides with white, the fencelines, the woods' edges, adding a dimension to the spring countryside, all soft, slowly darkening green, all yellow with dandelions and birch catkins! There were country roads leading into Sac Prairie in the days of my youth lined on both sides with thickets of wild choke-cherry — and wild plum trees — that on May days and nights filled all the roadway with their fragrance; they, more than anything before them, made one aware of the fullness of the season, signalling its height.

They made a bright demarcation between the brown and black fields; they leaned over brooks and ponds that gave back their bright wonder; they opened the woods, which before had been solid walls of green, breaking the rim of pasture and wood; they rode the crests of the hills, gnarled, twisted, broken — but always a great mass of showy blossoms, earth-bound clouds, starkly beautiful against the blue heaven — making the signature of May and flowering there all too short a time, under sun and cloud and by night under the moon, spectral in the land-scape, until the wind and the rain some too early hour scattered the fragile petals and ended their brief beauty.

With time and circumstances and inevitable change, the numbers of the trees—wild cherry, wild plum, wild apple—diminished, the trees were pushed back from all but the remotest country roadsides and fence-lines, cut down, poisoned—but all the woods could not stand against them, there along the rim of the forest they continue to blossom in their season, knowing, like man himself, an all too short hour of glory.

OF LATE MAY DAYS, sometimes almost on the edge of June, after all the other apple trees had done blossoming, the pink flowers of the wild crabapple unfolded in hill country around Sac Prairie. Already in my early years beginning to fade from the landscape before the opening of ever more fields, the wild apple which, as he passed along the southern extremity of the Sac Prairie country over half a century before, Thoreau had noticed "from the cars" marking the "handsome rose-colored flowers… remarkable for their delicious odor," was even then rarely come upon. "Half-fabulous," Thoreau had called the tree, and so it seemed when I came upon it in a thin woods or in a pocket of the hills, where sometimes a grove of the wild apple trees stood, shedding a haunting fragrance of great delicacy, an indescribable perfume that lingered in the nostrils and the heart, something that seemed more than the essence of that wild flower—a distillation of earth and time, something ancient that still celebrated its wildness in forgotten corners of the hills, unknown to most passersby, unrecognized, unsought and seldom found, though I sought it constantly, and with more success than Thoreau had had in New England, the Sac Prairie country being then wilder than Thoreau's in his time, not yet so crowded that the wild crabapple was forced to retreat or die. The hills gave it security, and cattle grazing there did it little harm. I found it from time to time, and looked upon it with great pleasure, and carried away from it a corymb of blossoms so that I might have its perfume so much longer than a visit to the tree assured me. I never saw it without a leaping up of spirit, as had I come upon something which had defeated time and change even as every man tries in vain to do.

IN WARM APRIL EVENINGS, the toads begin to sing along the Wisconsin, in the meadows and sloughs, in the marshes, the indigenous toad in the Sac Prairie area being *Bufo Americanus*, commonest of his species. Their pleasant, lulling trill falls so melodically to the ear that it is difficult to realize that a song of such liquid clarity and beauty could come from a creature so unlovely to look upon as a toad, as if the song were compensation for its warty skin and basilisk eyes.

No other nocturnal song quite matches it; the toads' steady trilling striking several, varied keys makes a choir that is an auditory delight not duplicated by nature in Wisconsin. They will not give voice in song until both warmth and humidity reach a desired level, never reached until April, and sometimes not until May; but once begun, the toads' songs can be heard throughout the night, throughout the spring, well through the summer, though a subtle change gradually comes over the song, a change in tone and tempo.

Toads' trilling makes a steady background of pleasant sound for songs and cries of birds and other batrachians celebrating the spring in the hot afternoons, the sultry evenings. The singing has a quality of peace and contentment, of continuity; however urgent it may be to the singers, it carries calm and temperance to the solitary walker in the night, imparting its contentment even as, by night, the whippoorwill spreads its loneliness and haunting nostalgia.

In spring, the song is companioned by many voices; in the summer nights it vies with tree frogs and wood ducks in the same milieu; the songs and cries blend, coming in and out of the dark, but it is the toads' trilling that lasts and lingers to assure the solitary walker that the life of the pond and the bottomlands is constant and eternal.

12

DURING THOSE EARLY YEARS of my struggle to make a living as a writer, while I tried my parents' patience and fortitude, working all day at pulp fiction with one hand and turning at evening to more dedicated writing, I used to refresh myself at night by walking up Madison Street—"the back street"—to Upper Sac Prairie, and across and down Water Street, which faced upon the river and the hills on the other side. West of Madison Street lay the open prairie, its darkness broken only by the stars overhead and the scattered yellow lights in houses dotting the fields and pastures; and east of Water Street shone more stars and the yellow window eyes at the foot of the hills across the river. These terrene lights to east and west, and the stars in the heavens above were for me in a real sense the limits of my universe, a universe in which the outposts of Concord and Baker Street and Walden Pond, of Spoon River and the *pays de Caux*, of Winesburg, Combray and Gopher Prairie, of Caerleon on Usk, Dickens's London, Egdon Heath, and Arkham, of Wuthering Heights and Frost's New England were no less remote than Venus gleaming on the western rim, despite such kinship as they bore to Sac Prairie.

This was the universe of the village, and I consciously avoided widening its horizons. Though I sought diligently to unroof the houses in Sac Prairie to examine the interiors, I stopped at speculation about the life that throbbed in the lamplit rooms at the edge of the prairie and the base of the hills; thus the perimeters of my universe remained a constant mystery, an enticement to which I was not in those years ready to yield because I enjoyed the promise of discovering in some future time the lives that were lived there, the promise of pushing beyond the immediate, intimate horizons to set up ever farther outposts.

In this world forever Arcturus rose over the northeast hills on spring nights and Orion strode across the southern heavens with the Dogs all winter long; the moon followed the sun's track among the stars; and on the one rim of that familiar shell the yellow lights beckoned to strange, unknown lives and the promise of Indian country and California and beyond them, the mysticism and color of the Orient; while on the other somewhere behind the looming hills, in winter like frozen thunder in their iridescence against the sky, lay not New York, but the country of Thoreau, of Emerson, of Melville, the New England of H. P. Lovecraft, Whittier, Hawthorne, and the open road of Walt Whitman.

These boundaries contained and satisfied me. I never felt the need to expand them in those earlier years, because there was so much to be learned in the small universe of Sac Prairie, and so little time in which to learn it.

AT SUMMER'S BEGINNING, the lindens—last of trees to bloom each year in Sauk Prairie—come to flower in a mass of pendant yellow blossoms, spilling their cloying fragrance into the hot summer afternoons along the streets of the village, invading rooms with their perfume. The first fruits of other trees and shrubs are already ripening—mulberries and raspberries have been picked, currants are reddening, and early harvest apples are taking shape for pies before July's end—when this last flowering occurs, stirring memories of linden blossom wine and linden tea, which were made in Sac Prairie for many decades before it became possible to walk into the stores and buy what one wanted without the labor of making it, however pleasant that labor might occasionally be.

While the last mock orange bloom and the flowers of the honey locust are fading, and the glory of the year's last blossom—the witch hazel—has not yet begun to bud, the lindens, with their heavy dark green leaves broken by the clusters of pale yellow flowers, make the last signature of spring in the lawns and along the streets of Sac Prairie, and their heady fragrance lingers in the summer air like some once and long-loved perfume out of the distant past, musty and sweet as the pages of an old album.

IN THE COUNTRY AROUND SAC PRAIRIE on autumn days the ghostly voices of spring rise once more. Suddenly one day they come to ear, after a summer of near silence, as were the vernal year indeed coming full circle, and then for a month, from September into November, these voices of spring will rise out of the familiar places as in March and April, repeating a pattern, lacking only the continuity of spring song—the *conqueree* of redwinged blackbirds, the garrulous conversation of grackles—sometimes seen by the hundreds in a grove of pine trees, the nostalgia of killdeers, flying low over the stubbled fields by night as well as by day, the threnodies of song sparrows—some of which will choose to remain in the willows along the brook and the river for the winter, the querulous caroling of robins, which is customarily a muted or broken parody of the spring song, the pensive chortling of bluebirds, the occasional songs of cardinals.

These are the voices of early spring, these and the batrachian runes of peepers, cricket frogs, tree-frogs, and toads, which also can be heard in autumn afternoons, sometimes from high on a hill far from pond or stream. A ghostly company, and save for grackles, never many in number in any given spot, their cries and songs are often muted, their melodies half-uttered, as if voiced in sleep, fretful and troubled, as were the migration or the hibernation not anticipated with pleasure. Of them all, the redwings are most numerous, most like their spring selves, with their whistling cries and the familiar *conqueree,* flying in many small flocks from place to place as if to bid farewell to the familiar stands, similar to their flight pattern in late winter and early spring; the grackles are equally as unchanged, continuing a colloquy begun with the turning of the year toward spring once more, as if but briefly interrupted by the responsibilities of propagating their kind. The bluebirds are obviously retreating, pausing only to forage around the Spring Slough trestle and the bridge over the east channel of the Wisconsin — the killdeers in mourning — and the robins, with their half-sung carols, their muted plaints, reluctant to take to wing again.

Even as in spring the colors of the opening leaves presage the colors of autumn foliage, so the cries and songs of birds in autumn recapture the spring. These are the last migrant voices to be heard; these will be the first to fall to ear when at last winter is done. For all the pleasure there is in hearing them again, there is a kind of sadness in their songs, the sadness that comes with the knowledge that they are diminishing into winter's silence, not swelling toward the choir of late spring and early summer.

But how they take possession of the autumn days! How welcome are their voices, and how readily they recreate the illusion of spring, fostered by buds already visible on barren twigs, by the perfumes, musks and pungences common to both spring and autumn! Together they create briefly again the illusion of March and April in October in the promise of spring just around the corner of winter.

A HOST OF SOUNDS, scarcely audible or so seldom repeated as to go all too often unheard, companion the well-known voices of the night—the low, cooing hoot of a long-eared swamp owl, the muted conversation of teal, the bell-like song of the saw-whet owl—existing on the very rim of awareness. Who, among the most solitary of night-walkers, common hears the quirting of whippoorwills, the mewing talk of muskrats, the voices of voles and meadow mice? Yet these sounds are everywhere in the spring and summer evenings, lost among the more commanding songs of birds and frogs, or so subdued as to be audible only to the waiting ear.

There are, too, the occasional unidentifiable sounds, the strange voices of uncommon birds or animals—of a migrant bird not native to the Sac Prairie country, stopping briefly overnight, or an animal long alien to this place passing through under cover of darkness, or the infinite small variations in the songs of little known warblers or frogs which lend a tantalizing strangeness to evening and night, rising out of the dusk and darkness of the woods and announcing that briefly an unknown visitor has paused in this familiar milieu, and will be gone again ere the inquiring eye can find him—of a bird little given to voice, like the black-crowned night heron whose barbaric cry rises now and then out of the slopes near the river. Such voices invest the night with something alien, but are not apart from the dark wood itself, for was not a dark wood forever the heart of mystery, the source of the unknown from the beginning of man's consciousness?—since it stood for the tangible foe of man as he conceived it: earth itself arrayed against his small fire and the multitude of his fears.

The night speaks with many voices in the thousand tongues of earth, not all known to the listening ear; each shouts its triumph in life into the enclosing womb of darkness, under the moons and stars and suns of this one infinitesimal galaxy in the cosmos; each throbs in harmony with the pulse of the night-walker passing by, of whom the habitants of the dark and darkening wood are often less aware than he of them. He may not know whence these voices come; he might be astonished to discover that the fluted piping making a choir of an April night in the meadows rises from a creature so small as to take three or four of them to cover the face of his watch; that the least breath of sound may come from the sleek, magnificent otter, a creature of size and power; that the ventriloquial voice of a screech owl rises not from many yards away but almost at his elbow; that the wild, sobbing scream from the high hills is the voice of the now rare wildcat.

The night is filled with voices—the sounds of gnawing, the songs of mating, the scuttering of passage, the screams of death, constantly, forever, the step of the night-walking solitary marking off another moment of his allotted time before he returns to dust which he will share in common with all the known and unknown habitants of the wood around him, all in due, inexorable time; the hyla choir no less than the whippoorwill's song, the jacksnipe's weird winnowing no less than the wild duck's whistling, the rabbit's death scream no less than the beaver's insatiable gnawing, the rustling of mice passing by no less than the weasel's remorseless pursuit, the love song of the woodcock no less than the proud high cry of the hunting hawk are all integral to the pattern of life and death.

NOT FAR DOWNRIVER from Sac Prairie the Ferry Bluff range marked off the southwestern horizon. There were four rounded heights—the long Ferry Bluff itself, with its stratified rock face looking northeast, the promontory of the Cactus Bluff, Seitz's Bluff, and beyond Andy Huerth's valley farm, Huerth's Bluff, making the dividing line between the massed hills there and the Genz Pocket beyond. A road led in to the old landing from which, years before, a ferry had crossed to Laws' Landing on the far bank of the Wisconsin, and from this point where the road ended a path wound up and across the face of the hills to the Huerth valley and the islands in the river there.

After returning to Sac Prairie from the city, I fell into the habit of walking at the bluffs to follow the path, climb to the promontory of Cactus Bluff, from which one could look far down the Wisconsin to where it bent westward in warm late autumn afternoons, sometimes alone or with Rikki, later with the children and their small friends, and on one happy occasion with Caitlin, lying on the hilltop to watch a mating pair of hawks high among the clouds on the sunlit blue heaven—in the hot afternoons the pungence of cedar and oak lay strong along the path, and the cries of gulls rose from the water far below, and the screams of hawks fell from aloft, while clouds rose majestically by, and the currents of the air, not to be felt so down along the river, moved ever restlessly on the hilltops—but more frequently by night, usually in solitude, to walk from the Ferry Bluff landing along the road to Walter Moely's sugar bush and again to the landing.

It was a place for meditation. The moonlit darkness—for it was a particularly inviting place, filled with mystery and the lure of unknown sounds, when the waning moon shone, its light falling alike upon the rock face of Ferry Bluff on the one side and on the other the stream of Honey Creek on its way to join the river—was filled with voices; the conversation of frogs, the cries of great horned owls in the bottomland woods, the lulling trill of toads, the rattling songs of summer cricket frogs making little choirs up along the river and on the banks of the creek, the nostalgic songs of whippoorwills, the *cree-ee* of wood ducks, the harsh cries of great blue herons foraging at the sandbars just out from the landing, and now and then, at rare intervals, the wild, startling calls of a single black-crowned night heron, widely spaced, so that each came suddenly, almost shockingly, like the voice of some rare winged creature from the remote past. In the spawning season, fish disturbed the waters of the creek close to its mouth with roiling sounds and abrupt loud splashes—none, however, as loud as the beaver's tail slapping the water to sound the alarm and notify his brethren that someone invaded the woods, a sound that came too with startling suddenness and could be heard well up along the creek on some nights, together with the gnawing of beavers eating bark from a tree bole or cut branch.

The highway went by half a mile to the north, and across the river the Yellowbanks road hummed with passing cars, increasingly as the years passed, but these sounds were peripheral and not commanding as the more intimate voices of birds and frogs and animals were in that place; and, walking there, I walked in a country all but shut away from the dwellings and works of my fellowmen. It was a place in which to indulge my solitudes — a place to pause for the green glowing fire-fly larvae in the grasses, shining forth, fading, winking out, and shining again — for the whispering passage of flying squirrels, which abounded there, nocturnal creatures never seen by day — to reflect upon the pattern of moonlight and shadow on the rock face of the Ferry Bluff that took rise near the sugar bush and could be followed around the hill all the way to the landing and a little past — to pause in a grove of moonlit trees and hear the wild geese honking by, following the river south or to the north, in season, while snow still lay in ghostlike patches up the slopes among the trees.

The bluff rose tall on heaven on the one side of the road and the path, and on the other — from the sugar bush to the landing — the widening stream of Honey

Creek and the massed woods of the bottomland, dense with blackness, and from the mouth of the creek to the south, the broad water of the Wisconsin giving back to the eye on quiet nights the stars, and on windy nights a scintillant moonglade. Not even at summer's height was the bottomland—or the hill—entirely silent—wood ducks gave voice once in a while, or a green frog, *Rana clamitans,* uttered its resounding, twanging song at intervals—or a whippoorwill gave a brief fluttering of calls and fell silent once more. If all else failed, the cries of the foraging herons rose from time to time off the bars in the river. The rustling in the grasses—of mice, voles, snakes and other lesser creatures, was as constant—if scarcely heard—as the movement of the air that could always be felt there, and, more rarely, the small sounds of raccoons fishing along the creek.

The day often disclosed fishermen along the shore not far from the landing that marked the end of the road leading in to the bluff area from the highway; but by night there was seldom anyone else there, save on weekends, when parties of college students from Madison came out to climb to the top of Cactus Bluff, and they were beyond hearing where I walked the road, forward and back, turning over in mind lines for poems, or the problems of the day, or the ties that bound me to those I loved, whether Rikki or Caitlin or the children, while the night and the moonlight and the sounds of life that rose all around—never obtrusively, but always with an air of privacy, for each of us is in his private world, however much those worlds impinged upon one another—soothed the troubled mind even as the multitudes of odors and perfumes gave pleasure to the senses, this nocturnal walking acting as the same kind of catalyst as a few hours spent sitting in the sunlight on the Spring Slough Trestle in the midst of a similar milieu did, affording the spirit nectar that was often more necessary than food for the body.

Ferry Bluff and its sister hills were little changed through the decades. The road was widened in a government project and invited more invasion, some of it unwelcome because of the detritus left behind, here and there trees were cut down—or fell, sometimes across Honey Creek, adding new water voices to the day and night—but, however much a scar might show by day, nothing of it was visible by night—the Ferry Bluff range, the road, the hillside path that led up under the ledge of Cactus Bluff and around and up to the crown of that hill with its magnificent view of the countryside north, east, and south, remained unchanged, offering by day the grandeur of the river valley and the Sac Prairie country on both sides of the broad Wisconsin, and by night the intimate, enclosed space in which to treasure my solitudes.

ON SUMMER DAYS the nighthawks made their erratic flights high above Sac Prairie and the countryside encircling the village, coasting down the sky at intervals, wings folded, to boom with wings spread and once again vault upward. In those days when I spent hours in the woods and marshes, I used to lie on the open hills watching them, taking pleasure in the quick, jerky propulsion that sent them among the purple martins and swallows ever to be seen against that blue heaven, watching them spiral aloft, crying, their harsh, nasal *peent* falling sporadically to ear, and the birds themselves often rocketing downward; and now and then I went looking for them and their nests—finding them sitting along the oak limbs like burls, so well protectively colored that often I did not see the bird at all until it took noiseless flight—finding the eggs lying among the stones of some promontory where sunlight fell upon them all day long while the birds kept to the air high above, foraging among the insects there.

They were most active in late afternoons and early evenings, when they came down from their blue heights to feed above the Wisconsin, over and under the bridges like giant moths, silent now, flying with their wide mouths agape, the stiff bristles that crossed their open beaks serving to keep out any object too large to be swallowed readily in flight. Sometimes as many as two score of them could be counted at the west channel of the railroad bridge, flying there deep into the dusk, among the swallows and chimney swifts and on occasion the whippoorwills, their cousins, foraging too. Their numbers seemed constant, save during periods of autumnal migration, when nighthawks by the hundreds and thousands came by on their way south during October and early November, often pausing to feed over the fields west of Sac Prairie, great batlike birds low over the earth in the twilight, evening after evening for perhaps three or four days, and then were on their way once more.

Slowly, as the wild hills and woods gave way before the expanding population, the nighthawks were seen with less frequency in the country; but as men moved into the nighthawks' country, into the moraine across the Wisconsin, into the low Ganser hills along the Mazomanie road—long their domain, from which they flew out to sky-coast and soar up into the evening heavens over the meadows and marshes—the nighthawks moved into the haunts of men. They found that the streetlights along Water Street in Sac Prairie attracted great numbers of insects, and they need only fly among them, make a few passes in one direction or another, to feed as amply as ever they had fed over the woods; they learned that the flat roofs of the commercial buildings on

Water Street were as ideal as any hilltop for laying and incubating eggs; and the village evenings now rang—as the countryside did not—with the cries and booming of nighthawks that coasted down the buttes of air above Water Street, as once over the valleys and the hills, filling the village evenings with the sound of the wild, bringing a little of the ever diminishing wildness into Sac Prairie, refusing to pass from among the ranks of men as so many birds have done before the spread of man's dubious civilization, but meeting and accepting the progress of man, perhaps to be here long after the human animal has vanished from the face of the planet.

I SAT FOR LONG HOURS at the Brook Trestle in the late winter and spring afternoons — and again in autumn, past mosquito-time, sat in the warm sun on one of the great beams that supported the trestle, much sheltered from any wind that blew, and with the constant, lulling music of running water companioning me. The Brook Trestle was not far from the Mazomanie road, for the railroad tracks ran parallel to that highway for most of the way between Sac Prairie and Mazomanie, and the sound of cars moving along the highway could always be heard in the background, though the trees that grew along the bank of the brook and the soft maples that towered over the trestle helped to shut away most of the sounds that filtered in from the road.

I sat there to read, to write, and to take the sun, as well as to keep a record, as it were, of the business of the woods in that place. There, very often, I heard the season's first bluebird, or saw the first skein of wild geese passing overhead, or glimpsed the first song sparrow in the willows, and responded to the wild crying of the year's first killdeer. I listened to the reedy conversation of redwings and bronzed grackles and took pleasure in the challenge of the crows or sometimes of the voices of a flock of gulls high over the leafing trees.

It was a solitary place except when the train went by on its way up into Sac Prairie, or down from it, shaking the woods in its passage and stilling all the voices of the wilderness, save only the raucous jeers of crows, and the high wild scream of a redtail hawk floating overhead. Such traffic as it knew was entirely in the water; muskrats came upstream now and then, busily engaged in exploring the banks at the water's edge—water striders danced with pennybugs on the brook's surface—rarely, an otter could be heard if not seen—painted turtles looked up out of the water from time to time, and frogs climbed up out of the brook to sit on the sun-warmed grass at the brookside, or hopped back in at the slightest hint of danger; though once in a while Clipper Niederklopfer came walking restlessly by on a round he had known for decades, freed from his winter's trapping, tired of his constant fishing, and stopped to talk for a little while before going on. Even more rarely, minnow-seiners came in along the brook and passed me by, on their way to the "deep holes where the minnies are."

It was a good place to be alone. I could meditate on any subject I chose, from some private dilemma to the condition of man in the mid-twentieth century, I could give uninterrupted rein to my imagination, I could set down verses or outline stories, listing as with the wind, while my eyes dwelt upon the yellowing catkins of pussywillows, hazel, and alder bushes, and hear the music of the birds—the talk of robins, the many songs of the sparrows, the gentle notes of purple finches, the urgent sounds of pileated woodpeckers and nuthatches, the ringing cries of tufted titmice, and sometimes the wild booming of jacksnipes aloft. The water flowed past as time ticked away, reminding me unceasingly of my own mortality, until it seemed that in that solitude I grew from youth to middle age, and nothing of change came to that little corner of Sac Prairie.

Once I reached the Brook Trestle, time lost its meaning. The hours went by uncounted, unnoticed, save only in the shadows that lengthened as the sun moved into the southwest corner, and the air grew a little more chill. How many poems came into being in that place! How much my view of Sac Prairie was expanded there!—while the brook flowed past to the Wisconsin, and, lost in that stream, to the Mississippi, and on to the gulf, and year after year the cress greened in that stream, the maples blossomed, bore fruit, and aged, and nature's clock ticked forever in the same key, involving me as certainly as it involved stone and bird, blade and tree.

HARVEST TIME in the years of my childhood was a time to gather the provender of the countryside, beginning with the appearance of oats shocks golden in the stubbled fields, ending with the first hard frost of autumn, though ours was not the grain in the fields, but rather the fruit and nuts that grew along the country lanes and roads.

When the wild black cherries ripened, we set off one Sunday afternoon—my father, my mother, my sister Hildred and I—in the Nash my father drove, together with a large piece of canvas, large enough to encircle a tree, spread out on the ground. My father could not resist any fruit or nut that came with so little effort to his hand, and the wild black cherries were the source of some of the wine he made, coming actually in the middle of his season—after dandelion and elderberry blossoms and before wild grapes were ripe enough to turn into wine.

We invariably rode west of town and seldom had far to go, for in those years the provender of the country was ready to hand along virtually every road; it was well before the baneful ingenuity of man had found a way to poison what grew along the line-fences and at the roadside; wild black cherries were easy to find, and at the first tree laden with fruit we came to, my father ran the car off on to the verge, and we all got out, my mother always a little fearful of snakes—though no dangerous snake could be found there. My father never lost time. In short order the canvas was spread out under the tree; then, with a sledge he carried, he gave the trunk a sharp blow—enough to bring down the cherries we could collect while he climbed into the tree and shook various branches to complete the harvest.

It was an altogether pleasant outing. To be in the open country, among the fields of waving or shocked grain, feeling the wind, smelling the fragrances of the countryside—of farmyards, black-eyed susans, yarrow, the sweet smell of the grass—to see my parents so obviously enjoying themselves in the harvesting of this early fruit—to know at one and the same time a feeling of freedom and of family harmony, that special unity all too soon lost with time and change, produced an euphoric happiness from which, with every new acquaintance with that wider world beyond the family circle, we were soon to be weaned away.

The outings for hickory nuts, butternuts, hazel nuts and elderberries were much the same. The canvas was employed beneath the nut trees, though hazel nuts were picked from the bushes, and elderberries were broken off to be taken home in boxes and bushel baskets, plucked from the stems, and turned into succulent syrup. The stain of berry juice lasted for days, that of hickory nut shells for longer and retained a little of the peculiar pungence so typical of the outer coverings. The harvesting was something that involved the entire family at the same time, and we took part in it with zest, though I suspect that no one's pleasure quite matched that of my father, who always took an especial pride of achievement in adding to the larder something so edible at so little cost as a few hours' time and a trifling amount of energy.

Alas! the countryside was soon despoiled. Roads and verges were widened, trees cut down, and in the end the bushes mercilessly sprayed with poisons by men too ignorant of their kinship with nature to consider the damage they wrought upon the land.

The time of the family outings passed—even the annual journey to Lohr's with sugar cane to be turned into sorghum, the one outing on which my mother did not accompany the rest of us, came to an end; the past claimed those pleasant hours and they did not come again. The cherry trees became rarities—though they could be seen blooming up the hill slopes far from the roads—ever fewer nut trees were to be found along the roadsides—hazel nut bushes and elderberries alike vanished before the poisons foolish men had devised to "improve" their habitat, and the very face of the earth west of Sac Prairie underwent a deteriorating change that signified a similar deterioration in the relation of man to his environment.

IN THE VILLAGE EVENINGS new moon and evening star often lay like great jewels low on the western slope of heaven, the thin cusp of the moon pale yellow, the bright gem of Venus or Jupiter or Mars a burst of brilliance, though it was the moon alone that was constant, the moon that filled the evening with its promise, the promise of adventure to come, of new days and nights to be lived, tranquil in that sky, with the dusk still lingering on the face of the earth, the sky still faintly rose and aquamarine, as if some fire still burned and glowed far down under the western rim, and the evening air fresh and fragrant, with the day's dust settled and a cooling exhalation rising from the leaves and the grass.

I loved these moonlit evenings not alone for the sight of the moon in that heaven, but for the sense of adventurous expectancy it conveyed, as if some profound revelation lay just past the moon, to be revealed on the far side of night, waiting on chance to be disclosed. On winter evenings the moon lay among the leafless trees like a last blazing blossom left from autumn, come later than November's last witch hazel; in the crisp dusks of early spring it danced among the lashing branches of the bud-thickened trees, making the wind's hushing sound in its nightlong rune.

I used to stand enchanted to watch the moon in its slow descent, watching its pale yellow deepen to chrome and ochre and red; or I walked along the railroad tracks to see it among the trees on its way to the horizon in the brief time it lay in the evening sky, taking delight in its beauty and the evening's tranquility, which soothed and calmed me, no matter what the day's tribulations might have been, and I was stirred by the promise, the adventurous expectancy integral to that twilight scene, enhanced in the village by the blossoming of the yellow streetlights reaching out to the prairie.

There were evenings on which the new moon shone that were so clear, so fresh, that it was as if the earth—and I, were still young, still untouched by the destructive hand of man, still beautiful with all the beauty of youth, before human greed despoiled the planet. It was in this that the essential magic of the new moon and evening star lay; it afforded a lingering return to the innocence of childhood.

2 1

EVERY SPRING I went in search of morels, sometimes day-long, whenever the weather permitted—and occasion-ally when it did not, hunting hills and woods, pastures and byways, from the time of the first *Morchella angus-ticeps* in late April to the fading of the last *Morchella crassipes* in early June, setting out early, when the grasses still hung with dew, and coming back often with the set-ting sun. I came to the hunting of these mushrooms by chance; not long after my return from an editorial posi-tion in Minneapolis, where I had spent such free time as I had at the Wandrei home, Donald Wandrei and his mother paid a visit to Sac Prairie, in the course of which I took them down to the Ferry Bluff to unfold for them the pleasant scenery of the riverside, and there the Wandreis, ardent mushroom gatherers, discovered growing within sight of the landing a score of prime *Morchella escu-lentas*. This introduction to the morel—followed by the tasting, confirmed me in the hunting, which soon became a pleasure I permitted nothing to diminish.

Perhaps it was as much the season of the year as it was the succulent quarry that took me from my desk into the woods, for it was the time of wild plum and cherry bloom, of violets and the first pungence of bergamotte that rose from underfoot where the hardy young plants were thrusting into May, of wild apples that stood like random clouds of pink and white in the middle of the green woods, of hawthorn blossoms with their cloying sweetness, of oak leaf pungence spilling into the south wind, of the last pasque flowers and the first yellow-orange puccoon, of mandrake and trillium and shooting stars, of the brook's voice singing through the vernal forest, the time of the height of odors and perfumes rising from the earth, from the musk of new-turned soil to the fragrance of opening leaves, of the spring glory of the trees, with the myriad shades of green that held in them the colors of autumn; and it was the time of migration for many birds, when I could be certain of seeing and hearing scarlet tanagers, prothonotary warblers and others of that family, rare least bitterns and seldom seen black-crowned night herons. And many an hour afield was spent watching the flight of hawks, in solitary majesty, or in mating play—observing the antics of kangaroo mice—satisfying the irrepressible curiosity of a bemused woodchuck—building a waterfall in a brook to increase and vary its voices—and in other such pastimes that enriched my spring days at the same time that they added to my larder, for the morels, which I gathered by the thousands each spring, were taken home to be strung up and dried, giving off at first a semenal musk that startled visitors, and at last a nut-like pungence very pleasant to come upon in the house.

Morels in numbers were not easy to find, though one memorable afternoon, while hunting with Donald Wandrei, I came upon an elm stump from the dying roots of which we collected almost a thousand morels; but for the most part morels grew sparely—two and three and perhaps a half dozen or twice that number around the base of diseased oaks, aspen, prickly ash, apple trees, and butternuts, where they could be found year after year until the host tree had either died or recovered its health, after which they were seen there no more; and I walked many days as much as ten miles to return home with but a few hundred of these flavorful fungi. The search led me over high hills and through deep valleys, through open woods and slopes covered with brambles and under-brush, along line-fences through cut-over land, into the marshes, and thickets of blackberries and poison ivy. It was not until the Dutch elm disease struck down the elm trees that morels were easy to find, but this very easiness lessened a little the challenge of the hunt, for all that it did not diminish the pleasure of the season. I carried the morels in a creel and a basket, scattering spores wherever I went, though few of them ever found a viable host.

What a sense of freedom was integral to those days! The earth never seemed more beautiful, with the wild plum and cherry trees making a lace of white along the woods' edge and marking out the fences dividing the black fields, while their perfume rode every wind; and the grasses in open places were yellow with dandelions, star-grass, and buttercups, and blue with the large bird-foot violets that grew profusely in many places; and in some hidden spots the tiny true white violet flowered and from its blossoms rose an ineffably delicate fragrance, though in time these beds vanished together with the wild crabapple that also gave forth a perfume that had no counterpart in the wild. It was still possible to see, when I began hunting morels forty years ago, farmers afield behind horses, making a kind of bucolic poem seen from a hillside, the dark field framed by pale green leaves and often white blossoms, and the farmer and his team moving steadily back and forth across, in silence broken only by the songs of birds or the alarm cries of chipmunks and blue jays and the occasional jeering of crows flying over.

These long walks into the countryside around Sac Prairie disclosed it as nothing else could have done. I learned where the whippoorwills nested, I chanced upon woodcocks and their young, I found where lady's slippers grew, and Indian pipes spectral in the dark woods, and showy orchids; I discovered badger digs, no longer common in south central Wisconsin, and knew where the redtails nested; I saw blue racers in the ecstasy of mating, unmindful of me, and now and then a gyrfalcon floating high in the blue or hunting the woods, rare birds and, rarer still, a great grey owl down from the far north. I knew where the brook was at its most amiable, from what heights the countryside was most gracious to the eye in its sweep over fields and mounds, past farms and hamlets, to the hills along the horizon.

I never tired of carrying the fruit of my labor, though my body protested on occasion at the unwonted exertion to which I put it, despite the manifest rewards offered by the countryside at every hand. These rewards were harvested, too, with the greater pleasure, and carried forever deep inside, a reserve of beauty to draw upon in darker hours.

SOMETIMES OF A SUMMER NIGHT the killdeers' wild crying echoes over the moonlit fields where the birds fly down the cornrows; all's silence save for the far, gentle calling of a long-eared swamp owl along the river—and this nostalgic crying that rings its changes through the dark, like the last voice of the prairie mourning the lost wilderness. It falls to ear out of the night, invading house, stabbing into the passing car, reaching to the solitary walker, companion to his solitude. The wild crying starts suddenly, rises to a crescendo as the birds sweep along low over the fields and pastures, and ends as abruptly, an echoing burst of primal sound, like something from the far past reaching tenuously into the present, the voice of the summer night in the immediate country bordering Sac Prairie, ringing out over crickets and katydids and the rustling of cornleaves in the wind. I never hear it without a quickening of the pulse, without the awareness of an answering within.

23

A HAUNTER OF THE MARSHES, of ponds, streams, sloughs, the bittern early enlisted my curiosity. "Thunder-pumper," the fishermen and trappers called it, for it sounded like a rusty pump when it gave voice—a strange, wild sound to rise from among the songs of redwinged blackbirds, robins, meadowlarks, bluebirds, and the resident and migrant members of the warbler family that made the same domain their own.

I heard it always with a kind of startled pleasure, for its cry rose without preamble, suddenly, sounded but a little while, and fell silent once more. For a long time I walked the railroad embankment that wound its way through the Wisconsin River bottoms without catching sight of that singer, but finally I made my way into the tall marsh grasses into the meadow where it nested, going with infinite care so that when at last I came within reach of that brown heron and settled myself to watch, I saw the odd way in which the bird drew back and twisted its neck and thrust it forward to make its three-noted call that sounded, as nearly as it could be transcribed, like *unk-a-dunk* to my ear. Once aware of the threat of danger—of my watching presence or of some passerby on the railroad embankment not far away—it squatted down and raised its long neck and bill straight up among the grasses, transforming itself on the instant into a semblance of a jagged old stump that would deceive all but that observer whose glance chanced upon the wary eye never entirely concealed in that stump-like form.

On wing, the bittern, like all of the members of its family, readily caught my eye, though it seldom flew as high in heaven as the great blue heron, largest of its cousins in Sac Prairie, but lost in the tall grasses of the bottomland, it was in a private world perhaps only a weasel or a fox could penetrate noiselessly. Certainly I could not, though I accomplished it a few times in the course of a decade, by dint of moving forward only when the bird was engaged in sounding its call, and then disturbed the bittern no more.

There were at one time perhaps as many as three or four pairs in the lowlands of the Wisconsin, audible from the trackbed of the Milwaukee Road spur that lay between Sac Prairie and Mazomanie, but these dwindled to one—change of habitat, the use of fatal or sterilizing pesticides, hunters careless of their quarry—any one of them might have been responsible for their decline in numbers; and that one is but infrequently heard in the upper reaches of the Lower Meadow beyond the brook that forms the meadow's northern and western borders. Its unmusical cry rings out unmistakably among the songs rising all around, and I listen for it in spring and early summer, and hear it as a communication from another world that is not quite as much my own as the world of hawk and owl, sparrow and lark.

SOMETIMES OF WINTER NIGHTS fog rolls up over the low-lands into the village from the Wisconsin and crystallizes on trees, dry weeds and blades, bushes, fenceposts, utility wires—transforming the countryside, so that in the morning the long-known landscape is a country made magic by the hoar-frost as much as an inch thick on every branch and blade, brilliant in the morning sunlight, gleaming and sparkling as with myriads of gems, and unbelievably beautiful against the blue dome of heaven before the warmth of the risen sun sends the frost crystals raining down like a fine fall of snow, a world in which purity has once again briefly resumed supremacy, and every vista that meets the eye is white and scintillating, and houses rise from the earth as in a land of dreams, into which the monsters of man's avarice, hatred, lack of integrity and responsibility, inhumanity and destructiveness could not reach, a world through which in wooded places deer and mice and foxes, rabbits and squirrels and even man walk as phantoms only briefly glimpsed in passing, through which rivers and brooks flow as in a land that never was, a world that lies before the eyes in such fragile, shimmering beauty that even a sigh might shatter it as with the force of a thunder-clap and destroy the crystal dream.

CARDINAL FLOWERS thrust their red spires out of the lush undergrowth of the marshes in midsummer, lining the shores of the Spring and Ice Sloughs and the banks of the Wisconsin's east channel, bringing a kind of light to these dark, shadowed places, particularly in the day's early hours when the morning sunlight fell upon them and made them to glow as were they akin to the wild balsam apple's creamy tapers that crowned the alders and willows nearby. They grew along the water's edge and in every wet swale, drawing the eye from afar when I walked the railroad bridge or the Spring Slough Trestle, framing the dark water for many weeks, for the red lobelias shone throughout the day as were some part of the morning sunlight caught in the tall spires, and the flowers opened up the stem, so that the last blossoms crowning the spike of flowers glowed scarlet when the first tubular blossoms had faded.

And when at last they were done, their scarlet gave place to the dark blue of closed gentians. Neither cardinal flowers nor closed gentians were plentiful, having already in my early years begun to die away from the invasion of man and his works. Cardinal flowers and gentians saw the summer into autumn in the marshes. I used to count them, marking their dwindling numbers with sadness, though now and then I was elated to find that their numbers had increased. Of the two, the gentians were the more numerous; they were hardier and withstood the thrust of man more readily, and could be found on drier land as well, where the cardinal flowers would not grow, though their favorite habitat remained moist ground and they shone out of the grasses all the way along the railroad tracks toward Mazomanie where the ditches offered more moisture than upland country. Neither was as much to be seen as penstemons and the loosestrifes, the wild balsam apples and the dusty rose of Joe Pye weed that covered the upper reaches of the uncut Lower Meadow for a long time every autumn. I always saw them with pleasure as the ultimate fruiting of the marshes before the time of ice and snow.

BEFORE THE WIDESPREAD USE OF PESTICIDES decimated their numbers, migrating hawks passed high over Sac Prairie in late autumn, broad wings flying wide apart, hundreds — on occasion, thousands — of them, circling and soaring, drifting slowly southward. I used to lie on a hilltop to watch them pass by, seeing hawks sometimes from one horizon to another flying and riding the air-currents on motionless wings, in circles within circles, interwoven, spreading apart, knitting together again, silently going past, beautiful against the sunny sky, moving leisurely into the south, possessing heaven.

Warm, sunny October days brought them down from the north. They traveled without haste, sometimes pausing to circle and soar and float above the same hill or valley for as much as half an hour at a time before moving on, none foraging, only riding the currents of the upper air high above the earth, as if enjoying their mastery of the sky. Their numbers seemed endless; they had drifted past by two miles to the ridges against the southern horizon, and they were still taking shape out of the north, an unending flock of birds unfolding across heaven.

I never saw them without a racing pulse and a lifting of the heart.

THE WINTER MARSHES drew me on temperate days of thaw.
I went in along the brook from the Mazomanie road,
crossed the Brook Trestle, and followed the brook bank to
the ash-grown place where it emptied into the east channel
of the Wisconsin. The path I took was open to the meadow
on the south and walled off on the north by woods and
underbrush on the far side of the brook, a woods thick
enough to hold off the north wind and leave the meadow
side of the brook warm with pooled sunlight.

All along the brook rose the subdued voices of the
meadows—the whispered songs of the tree sparrows
and juncos, the cries of tufted titmice, the *phe-be-be* of
chickadees, the warnings of blue jays, the occasional
threnody of a song sparrow that elected to remain for
the winter, the melodies of purple finches, the complaints
of robins which, too, chose not to migrate and made a
small flock of birds that fed on the berries and seeds so
plentiful in the lowlands, vying for food with the mice
and voles that climbed the reeds for seeds, and left tracks
in the snow that told of urgent need and sometimes—in
spots of blood, fox tracks that ended in pouncing marks,
or the print of owl's wings—of sudden death.

Across the meadow crow caws rang out in the crisp winter air and echoed against the hills that rose into the eastern sky beyond the meadow and the Milwaukee Road spur that bounded it on that side, while from the woods rose now and then the scream of a red-shouldered hawk, an eruption of calls from a group of barred owls, the high, challenging notes of a pileated woodpecker, the drumming of a grouse, a rare gyrfalcon's cry or a king-fisher's rattle where he flashed along the brook.

Sunlight lay mellow on the snow-covered meadow, coming out of the low southern sky, gleaming from blades of grasses that stood above the snow, and height-ening the color that abounded all winter long in the lowlands—the red osier wands, the mustard willows, the maroon of soft maple buds that arbored the path beside the brook—and the fruit on which the smaller birds fed: orange bittersweet, the brown, beautifully sculptured climbing false buckwheat seeds, the clustered dark blue carrion berries, the cerise fruit of the burn-ing bush or wahoo, the coral berries ranged thickly on the twigs of the black alder and shining out of the dark woods even at a distance like pale red torches, sweetbri-ar's dark blue fruit, and the red rose haws that stood in many places, in and along the meadow. Great old maple trees grew on the western rim of the meadow out of a swale there; beyond them the brook meandered through a region orange with a thick growth of bittersweet twin-ing among the prickly ash, and, under an old black ash, opened into the river.

I became accustomed to sitting at the sunlit base of the most open of the maples, facing south, to read and write, far removed from my fellowmen, occasionally startling a deer or a passing hawk, jeered at by crows, with the meadow unraveling to the south and the distant woods there, and at my right the trees crowded between the meadow and the river, while to the east the meadow reached to an old haybarn there, beyond which the tall, snow-clad hills lay on the sky like frozen thunder; and, tiring of this place, went up along the drainage ditch that divided the meadow there to sit at the south wall of the old barn, which on a day of thaw gave off all the fragrance of June in the perfume of the hay that came out between the warped, old, unpainted boards of its walls. I spent many winter hours there, sitting on a spill of hay left behind by the farmer who came now and then throughout the winter to haul away a load of the summer marsh's yield, taking the sun, writing—principally poems, none of any great merit, however pleasing they seemed to eye and ear.

The brookside path and the adjacent meadow were places of singular tranquility—a domain of mouse and crow, rabbit and fox, of vole and shrew and hawk, tranquility that the passing train not only did nothing to disturb but actually seemed to enhance, winding its way along the tracks from the south and through the woods over the Spring Slough Trestle on the way into Sac Prairie like a great beast with box-cars and caboose colored red and green, yellow and orange, chuffing past and rattling through that lowland like any inhabitant of the country, its whistle echoing flatly over the meadows like the distant lowing of cattle at the Lenson farm along the highway east.

Here on some day in late winter, while snow still patched the earth, the first spring voice would sound — a killdeer's wild *kildee, kildee,* where the bird flew in low over the meadow out of the south — a redwing's *con-queree,* rising from the meadow's edge along the railroad embankment, where that black, glossy bird with its bright shoulder patch swayed on a catkin-pearled willow — the shrill *ee-ee* of a march harrier — the high cry of an osprey, now but rarely seen — the chortling song of a bluebird flying over — the mimetic sounds of starlings; and along the brook muskrat and mink and beaver would once again set about the business of living, while high in the blue the wild geese would fly over in great arrows and wedges, honking their way north; and the meadow would soften and the brook overflow to shut away the meadows from me until summer firmed the earth once more, the water returned to within its banks, and I to the hills.

THE STILLNESS OF LATE WINTER NIGHTS is often broken by one voice, that of the long-eared swamp owl, whose soft, cooing hoot falls gently into the deepening dusk, more like the voice of a dove than of an owl, and rising again before dawn, coming with that ventriloquial quality common to many owls, so that the bird seems always much farther away than it is.

I used to hear it calling, I thought, from the upper reaches of Heiney's Slough when I walked the railroad tracks, though it was nearer; and sometimes lying abed in the early hours of the morning, before dawn, I hear it sound—evidently from the marshes half a mile to the south—though the bird cried from out of the trees immediately adjacent to the house—an intimate sound that opens the night-held woods and the night itself for a little while, a fragile shell of sound enclosing the night outside and what is left of day within and, too, promising the light beyond the dark.

That solitary voice coming out of the dark woods renews that bond, seemingly so tenuous, in reality so strong, to that world of nature of which I know myself an integral part, at that hour when the familiar face of the daily world has fallen to darkness, leaving no barrier between.

ON THE NEAR EDGE OF SUMMER in wasteland areas—
sandy roadsides, open hillsides of sandstone and shale,
dry banks in lowland places and along the railroad right-
of-way, the pale yellow blossoms of the prickly pear open
their waxen petals and turn sunward, petals framing the
intricate stamens, like miniature suns making light of
their own among the satellite flowers of spiderwort and
blue vervain and the last of lupines, wild roses and dog-
bane, yarrow and goat's rue and meadowsweet—the
only cactus to grow in the country around Sac Prairie,
protected from wanton hands by spines and tufts of bristles and so left untouched to spill its delicate, fruitlike
fragrance into the hot June and July afternoons, slowly
taking over the waste places and making these sandy
banks and slopes brightly beautiful for a few brief weeks
every year, places where, in late autumn and winter, tall
bracted mullein stalks make miniature saguaros in the
dry and rocky country of south central Wisconsin.

Prostrate plants, the prickly pear seldom catches the
attention of the casual passerby, and is glimpsed only at
its height of flowering from passing cars. The solitary
walker knows it best. I used to seek it out before I knew

how common it was in the surrounding countryside, and sometimes dare the spines and bristles to carry a single blossom home so that I might have its warm beauty under eye for longer than I could view it passing by.

How the blossoms glow off roadsides and the railroad tracks! — lighting a world of their own, spined and guarded against the hand of man, ever raised against natural beauty in all its forms.

30

IN THE SHALLOW PONDS west of the village on some night late in March rises the first batrachian voice, announcing winter's end and the advance of spring once more, in an ancient pattern that was old before man made his appearance on the planet. I go out nightly before and after the vernal equinox, waiting to hear that first, quavering, uncertain note—either of the spring peeper, *Hyla pickeringii* or *crucifer,* or the spring cricket frog, *Hyla gryllus*—rising, if not out of Henn's Pond on the near side of Otter Creek, then out of Patterson's, a mile away across the stream—both shallow bog-ponds, not deep enough to last out the summer except in wet seasons.

Sunlight falls on both through the day, melting snow and ice, warming the earth so that the *hylidae* can come up out of the frost-free bogs and salute the spring that is never very far away. Their primeval cries are symbolic of that resurgence of life, of earth's rising from the long winter sleep, of man's survival through another cold season, and my own therefore, that inevitably follows upon the long season of cold and ice, of winter death.

Hard upon that first uncertain voice sounding so tentatively in the chill night come its companions—the one voice grown to a score, the score to a multitude, among which are the croaking of the woods frog, *Rana sylvatica,* and the chuckling of the pond frog, *Rana pipiens,* by which time the spring is well advanced, March has given way to April, and winter is already far behind.

Nothing exceeds the delight that takes rise in the first batrachian voice coming out of the still crisp darkness. I have waited under many a clouded heaven, in rain, under new moon and evening star, beside the still leafless trees black on heaven, in the quiet windless, chill air to hear that first frog call, to know renewal once again, to meet one more spring.

I NEVER FOUND THAT NATURE FAILED ME in the continuity of time and place so necessary to my well-being. While the condition of man on his planet slowly worsens, the pattern of the seasons changes not at all, however much nature's aspects reflect the damage wrought by man in his avarice and his devotion to false, unnatural values.

After every winter, there comes a day when the first frog begins to sing, when the first killdeer's nostalgic cry rings out over the still snow-patched meadows, when the vanguard of the redwings sing from the willows and the first threnodies of the year's first song sparrow rise from the brookside, the wild geese go honking over into the north, and the caroling of robins and the keening of mourning doves fill the village evenings between sundown and dark, when the catkins pearl the willows and aspens. The sere, snow-covered earth gives way to green, the green makes place for the deep yellow of buttercups and cowslips, the blue of squills, pasque-flowers, irises and violets, and leaves spill their subtle musk into the sunny afternoons, and life burgeons again.

In the village as in the country, birth and death know no winter; here life is more patently unceasing change.

Familiar faces vanish, long-known voices sound no more, gone to ground. The young grow up to confront a life ever more complex, and in their time are harried to the grave, scores of men and women who may never see the beauty of the earth they live in, who may never know themselves as integral to nature.

I walk among them, it often seems, increasingly an alien informed by compassion and understanding, but less content among my fellow men than in the marshes or the hills, on the river or along a country road at night, where I am closer to coming full circle, to awareness of that ultimate darkness that is the merging of the self with time and the inevitable dust.